Free Verse Editions

Edited by Jon Thompson

Extinction of the Holy City

Selected Poems

Bronisław Maj

Translations from the Polish by Daniel Bourne

Parlor Press
Anderson, South Carolina
www.parlorpress.com

Parlor Press LLC, Anderson, South Carolina, 29621

Library of Congress Cataloging-in-Publication Data on File

978-1-64317-457-0 (paperback)
978-1-64317-458-7 (pdf)
978-1-64317-459-4 (ePub)

1 2 3 4 5

Cover art by Wojciech Kołyszko. Used by permission.
Book design by David Blakesley.

Parlor Press, LLC is an independent publisher of scholarly and trade titles in print and multimedia formats. This book is available in paperback and ebook formats from Parlor Press on the World Wide Web at https://www.parlorpress. com or through online and brick-and-mortar bookstores. For submission information or to find out about Parlor Press publications, write to Parlor Press, 3015 Brackenberry Drive, Anderson, South Carolina, 29621, or email editor@parlorpress.com.

Contents

From *Family Album (Album rodzinny)* and *Extinction of the Holy City (Zagłada Świętego Miasta)*

From *Weariness (Zmęczenie)*

From *Light (Światło)*

From *Such Freedom (Taka wolność)*

Chile

Rain Outside the Window, and a Glass of Tea: An Introduction, Years Later, to the Poetry of Bronisław Maj

Perhaps the most interesting "political poetry" to emerge out of the last generation of Polish poets who came into print during the Communist era was that of Bronisław Maj—not because it referenced its current climate of individual and cultural oppression in a topical or obvious way—an atmosphere in which Poland increasingly became split between "official" and underground/black market spheres of activity—but because this poetry above all seemed to address the integrity of the poetic gaze itself. Often a Maj poem will double back on itself, to wrestle with whether he got it right, or to address the vulnerability of the past, always at the mercy of whatever future is writing the history. His poems thus contain a scrupulousness and second-guessing of seeing, coupled with an acute awareness of the fragility of memory, of the erasures challenging cultural continuity, and, above all, the vulnerability of those trying to cope with both the everyday and the eternal. In this enterprise, Maj brings to the poem an amazing ability to combine the immediate with the universal, the lyrical with the metaphysical:

> Rain outside the window, on the table a glass of tea,
> a lamp glowing. Naïve, but that's how I see you
> in five, twenty, a hundred-twenty years as you read
> this poem and think about me, from a generation
> or a century ago.

The lyric moment expressed in the opening to this poem—initially seeming to just contemplate a quiet day of rain coupled with a few creature comforts—suddenly turns into an earnest rumination about the impossibility of communication, about the fear of being erased, and ends with a hope of reaching this future reader through "the common language / of our five / immortal senses."

In a more political context, this epistemological scrutiny, not just of the word but of how the world gets written about—in which Maj always seems to judge his own poetic attempt as wanting—is especially refreshing given the polarized rhetoric elsewhere at the time, where both state and anti-state seemed to be so assured that they alone possessed the truth. But not that Maj sought political compromise; instead, it was to sound an alarm. Indeed, much of his poetry from the 1980s, as it both interrogated and mourned the

ongoing physical and spiritual deterioration of Poland in general but espe-
cially his beloved Kraków, certainly shows this interweaving of the tangible
with the metaphysical. The world around him was falling apart; literally,
given the effects of pollution pouring down from the surrounding ring of
factories and mills on the centuries-old bricks of the Holy City of Kraków,
located as it was in a bowl surrounded by those industrialized hills. "This city
has died," begins one of his untitled poems, whereas in "Another Dead Lan-
guage" we encounter this worrisome recognition of a disintegrating world
taking place in the bricks of language itself:

> Instead of air,
> always fog, and in the fog, someone speaks to me—
> perhaps in Polish. I can make out
> words, but I don't understand the sense.
> It has already crumbled. Maybe
> it's because he is speaking some other language
> that has already gone extinct.

Even more alarming is the vision in his poem, "Maybe it will happen in
the span of a sentence. . ."]. It starts out on a common theme for Bronisław
Maj, about the witness of poetry to our day-to-day lives, and the necessary
freedom of the poet to notice this transpiring world. But then, several lines
later, a word creeps in—in Russian rather than Polish—and as the poem
progresses other Russian words replace Polish words here and there until the
very last lines of the poems are entirely in Russian. At the time of composi-
tion, this "invasion" of Russian into Polish in this poem was a very pointed
expression of Maj's fear of Russian Sovietism overwhelming the Polish lan-
guage as it was also threatening to overwhelm Polish life itself. In Maj's own
subtle, organic way, however, rather than decrying this "language-snatch-
ing," he instead captures it in the very act.

Since I first read this poem back in the late 80s, I've been captivated
by its gripping fusion of form and function, but how to translate it? To use
Russian as invading non-Slavic English would just look incomprehensible
(despite the precedent of the narrative language of Anthony Burgess' 1962
novel *A Clockwatch Orange* with its horrowshows, droogs, devotchkas and
viddy this and viddy that, suggesting that England was once again invaded
and its language yet again altered—this time by a Cold War foe). Using Ger-
man wouldn't work either, since German is hardly "dangerous" in any way
to contemporary readers of English (nor is it as close to English as Polish is to
Russian), while using Spanish would send a completely wrong message polit-
ically, since I am hardly worried about Spanish swamping English. Another

factor, too, is that the Cold War ended: Poland held its first free elections in 1989, the Wall came down, and Soviet troops left their main occupying base in Legnica with hardly a trace remaining of their presence. Nowadays, Kraków is relatively environmentally-protected, brightly painted, and open to the travelers of the world.

But, in the past year, with Russia now threatening Ukraine, including a decided attempt to subsume if not obliterate its language and literature, I turned once again to this poem. It indeed speaks not just to one time and one place, but to a wider, and unfortunate, dynamic of the world. Thus, in the end, I did try to translate it, deciding to put the "invading" words in italics, and to rely on a lengthy translator's explanation like this one to provide context.

Born in Łódź in 1953, Bronisław Maj as an adult soon came to make his permanent home in Kraków, where he taught contemporary literature at Jagiellonian University as well as emerged as a major poet of his generation. In 1983 he received the Sęp-Szarpiński Prize for younger Polish poets, in 1984 he was awarded the Kościelski Literary Prize, given each year by the Geneva-based Kościelski Foundation in recognition of outstanding younger Polish writers, and in 1995 he was given the PEN Club Award for poetic achievement. Over the years he has published numerous collections of poetry, perhaps the most significant of which were the untitled poems in *Wspólne powietrze* (*The Same Air,* Wydawnictwo Literackie, 1981) and *Album rodzinny* (*Family Album,* Oficyna Literacka, 1986), the former published officially in Poland's culturally and politically torn 1980s (a period, as I mentioned before, significantly ripped apart between the last throes of Communist control and the growing power of the Solidarity-connected independence movement), while the latter publication appeared in the country's underground press. And, indicative of the growing publication complexity—and international reach—of Polish poetry in the 1980s, both books were also published in 1986 in a single edition in London by the Polish emigré press, Puls, under the title *Zagłada świętego miasta* (*Extinction of the Holy City*).

During the mid-to-late 1980s, Maj was also the editor/director of *Na Glos* (*Out Loud*), a Kraków reading series which served as one of the few "legal" literary forums available to the many Polish writers who chose not to belong to the government-controlled Polish Writers Union, including such figures as Wisława Szymborska, Zbigniew Herbert, Urszula Kozioł, and Marek Nowakowski. Since then, however, Maj has published much less, and to a large extent become removed from the literary scene. In 1986 itself, along with his longer collection *Family Album/Extinction of the Holy City*, he also published a shorter volume of poems, *Zmęczenie* (*Weariness,* Wydawnictwo

Znak), but onwards it was a long wait for his next work, a hiatus that in some ways corresponded with the Polish culture's own troubles in finding its voice in the transitional period from Communism to the dog-eat-dog world of Poland's first "free market" years. Then in 1996, *Światło* (*Light*, Wydawnictwo Znak) finally appeared. Maj has published further collections since then, including an ironic memoir, *Kronika wydarzeń artystycznych, kulturalnych, towarzyskich i innych* (*A Chronicle of Artistic, Cultural, Social, and Other Miscellaneous Events*, Wydawnictwo Literackie) in 1997, and a collected works, *Elegie, treny, sny (Elegies, laments, dreams*, Wydawnictwo Znak) in 2003.

For my part, except for "Maybe it will happen in the span of a sentence . . . ," most of my work in translating these poems and publishing them in American literary journals occurred in the late 1980s and into the 1990s and early 2000s. It was in the mid-1980s, when I was living in Poland on a Fulbright Fellowship for work on the translation of younger Polish poets, that I first had the pleasure to get to know Bronisław. I had already been very much taken by his poetry, and I was so grateful that he was willing to meet with me, to answer my questions, and to make suggestions about how I was shepherding his words into English. One memory I have of visiting his apartment on the edge of Kraków's Old Town was an unwashed tea-glass that he kept sitting on a bookshelf. It was a shrine to Bronisław's "Mistrz," the "Great Master" in the eyes of many poets of his generation: the 1980 Nobel Prize-winner in literature, Czesław Miłosz, who had visited Maj in his apartment during one of the first of Miłosz's trips to his slowly "thawing" homeland during his years-long exile in the West. Such an endearing gesture to keep this one small artifact representing a passing onward of the poetic torch, but also a sign of Maj's ongoing desire to preserve even the little things of the world—especially when they might hold such bottomless depths...

—Daniel Bourne, Wooster, Ohio, November 19, 2023

P.S. A final bibliographical note. In organizing the selected poems for this volume of Maj's poetry in translation, I have grouped the poems mainly in accordance with the books in which they first appeared in Polish. I start with his two most important collections, *The Same Air* and *Family Album/ Extinction of the Holy City*, followed by selections of his later, shorter collections, *Weariness* and *Light*. The final two sections are out of chronological order, however, providing selections from his early poetry from the 1970s (published in *Such Freedom*) as well as the long-poem *Chile*, which appeared as a separate part of *Family Album*, but is a distinctly different poetic work. Indeed, *Chile* is perhaps the single example of Bronisław Maj directly addressing political oppression, although with a title displacing it to another "backyard" of oppression (to borrow Timothy Garten Ash's terminology) in Pinochet's right-wing totalitarian state of 1980s Chile. Whether Maj chose to name the poem this way in order to avoid possible censorship in Poland, or to show solidarity with the writers of Latin America suffering their own brand of repression, is open to debate.

Extinction of the Holy City: Selected Poems

From *The Same Air* (*Wspólne powietrze*)

Is it right of me to keep rummaging
through time, forever behind me? And when
can I begin? The train pounds
on its journeys while I stand at the window
with my face to the wet air. I see
sleepy towns rise up in an instant—
and disappear so quickly they were never
there. So how much longer will these fields continue,
bathed in sunlight, swarming with people and animals—
August the time of harvest in my country. This passage
before my eyes of complete and independent forms of life—
when do I have the right to begin? The same right
that anyone has, who has just caught sight of something
he knows he can never own. Life under the sway
of the year's four seasons, the unrestrained
seasons of the heart, Sunday
in a small town.

An afternoon in August. This far away we can hear
the rush of the sunlit Raba. We can see the mountains,
my mother and I. Such clear air.
Each black spruce on Mt. Luboń stands out
as if it grows in our own garden.
Such an overwhelming sight. It surprises my mother
as it does me. I am four years old. I don't know
what it means to be four years old. I'm happy
and I don't know what the word *happy* or *to be* means.
I just know my mother is here with me.
She experiences what I experience. And I know for a fact
that this evening
as with every evening, we will go
for a long walk in the woods. Any moment now
and we will start.

The train station at night. The shell of stone
and icy air, the wind slamming through the doors,
the fluorescent bulbs overhead. This bag lady
from the City Gardens spends her winter here. I have
just bought my ticket and in two hours
you will open the door. I will say I am freezing
and need something to eat. Already I feel the heat
of your breath on my shoulder. Just then the bag lady
comes back into view. It could be you here in her place,
but it's not. And no one, absolutely no one,
is guilty. That is just the way it happens, you breathing
evenly and safely by my side, the way it happens
that I am so happy, thanks to God, thanks to whomever
I have to thank: to every breath wrenched out of despair
from the walls of this great icy vacuum
where nothing but the wind
can keep itself alive.

On her way out this morning, she left
the lilies of the valley, their dark scent
of last night filling the room. Satiated,
I look out on the hard sweat of the Vistula,
workers pulling the coal barges through the locks
without a motion to waste, speaking no more
than they have to, for the most part a gesture
of hands. The barge moves off downstream, laden
with its touchable cargo of the senses. If, in spite of this,
I insist I will write a poem, then no word must be wasted
to bring these simple goods across: the river,
the smell of flowers, the movement of a hand
understood by two people, and finally the eye noticing
everything that happens. This
is all there is to it. Only this
remains beyond our ken.

I will never write a long poem. Everything
I have ever known tells me
it would be a lie. This world goes on
between two gulps of air; in a single glance,
a quick contraction of the heart. And I
can only be in one place at a time—with that
which is with me now, good for only
ten or fifteen lines, a poem short as the life
of a garden butterfly, the glint of light on a wave,
on a cathedral, or on a human face. Ten or fifteen lines,
and that, which exists between them: the light
which does not end, the garden butterflies
which will be with us forever, the human journey
to death and beyond.

The world is a still life, giving no sign
it is living, giving no sign at all. The fact
the doorstep squeaks beneath your feet
shows the wood is warped, nothing more.
It squeaks. There is no complaint it is making.
No warning it gives. No need to see everything
in the guise of a symbol. No stubborn investigation
into the connection, no bolstering of one's confidence in
what is here and now. Things
do not need crutches. They live
without doubt or support. No stone depends
on a worn-out metaphor about a heart. While we,
separated—lost—get cut
on all the jagged edges, bleed from our contact
with splinters, with blade. But let
there be this one kinship between us—
even though this is a kinship
of blood.

Probably he can only see
In shades of gray. At night he wakes me
howling at the unseen moon.
When we meet in the ·doorway, his body
dances in delight. My words
dance with a delight of their own. But I know
we are not dancing together. I know
his coat turns yellow, red, crimson, I know
he sees it as a change of gray. Maybe
gray is the only color. Maybe
the full moon is the only true god. But I
am the one who controls his leash. It is I
who will decide, certain
I am the last of my line. Just as he
is certain everything ends with him. I look
deep into his yellow eyes. Behind
their glass boundaries,
opens the void from whence we came,
and from which we still come
gnawed
to the very bone.

I lie in the meadow, my face
deep in the grass. High above us
floats a lark. On top of my hand an ant
tugs on a dry stalk. I see
through its eyes: the chasms
in the pores of skin, the wilderness
of grass, the treacherous wasteland
in a granule of sand. The ant flounders
in the salt and sweat dripping from my eyes.
From up there, where the lark is,
we all look the same
as we hug the earth: I,
the ant, the yellow flowers. The lark
is rising even higher. Approaching truth
or getting further away.
And if there is more than one truth,
the truth of lark or ant, of song
or crawling, of sky or hand, which one
will win me—here on the sideline
I can't escape? I am lost in this mania
for contrast, one superfluous question
after another, caught
in this cowardly in-between, my own truth
always slipping from my grasp.

Why is it that in my world
You don't exist? Why can't I see
the trace of Your hand
in the inhumanly solid construction
of a blade of grass? For me
this song of the blackbird
has no master. I can't hear
You listening. There is no voice
rising up through the day's clamor.
And at night, submerged in the awesome breathing
of the darkness, I feel that everything happens
with me as the source. Between my body
and the blinded star above my head there runs
an icy road of panic, its measure
of the infinity that begins and ends with me.
One step further—and I can't see a thing.
Is it because I have no faith in sight
that I can't see? It could be
that what I experience is only
a recurring hunger for a glimpse,
and there is nothing else than this hunger
rising up in the clamor of the day,
inside the cathedral of a blade of grass,
underneath the vacuous eye of a star.

A dragonfly pinned to the trail
with my foot. Why did I do that? But
it was all quicker than thought: the spark
of flight, the jut of my foot
and death. Death. I can see
the body ground into dust. My own body
hums, the muscles filled with energy
like a flexed young branch, my unerring
eyes. Youth, strength, and their confirmation
through death. I will keep on traveling
with this thorn. No,
I'm not thinking of what in time
will be done to me. Rather
I'm afraid of my own body,
its reactions quicker than my mind.
The fact that in this world
it is all I have.

Evening, a burning campfire, the outgoing rings
of light. Beyond its edge there is nothing. Only we
in the center are alive: our loud shouts, songs,
laughter. Soon, the wood will burn down,
the flames cough. With the same words
we describe the gasps of a dying man. Always
there lingers something of the fire. Only later
will we realize there was nothing. Only darkness
in which we make out the few things that remain:
our faces, suddenly changed, bending down
over this one spot of earth, the black figurines
of the trees, the sky turning a little more light,
and the cold glint of the stars. And no one knows
why we have remained silent for so long, why
when we speak our first words
are whispers.

Whenever he described to me this park, this pathway,
a weak flame broke out in his watery eyes. His voice deepened
and his hands stretched out as if
with a piece of candy. He told me
the squirrels would race to his palm
without fear. Now it is I
who stand here, every detail
the way he remembered it:
the dark tunnel of poplars, the insects
chattering, the cuckoo bird and yellow forsythia.
This place became a part of him forever,
his memory faithful to the last leaf, this place
where not a trace of his passage
remains. The inhuman, perfect beauty
in the midst of which he died
never had need of him. It needs
no one. Neither then nor now. It just
is, and will always be the same. On the path,
another squirrel, the twentieth generation
that he fed by hand, flees
in a headlong sprint, scared to death
at my approach.

Quiet apartment in which someone lies dying,
the careful closing of doors, the whispers, the short sobs
stopped by a handkerchief. The smell of medicine
no longer needed, the death candle's yellow flame.
My father stands there speechless. Just a boy
whose mother is dying. No one can yet believe
in what is happening, in what, hidden from us all,
already happened. Still, everyone
keeps silent. In the courtyard someone thumps on a rug,
a car engine races. An argument on the stairs, music.
A breeze blows in through the window the smell of mown grass.
It smothers the candle. Nothing here
is any of her business. Nothing remains
To link her with us. We stay. Already
we are able to burst into tears, loud, louder—
at our own unceasing witness
to life.

Strange evening, I sit in the garden, the pines
still sharp against the sky. The neighborhood mothers
call their children home. In the distance
a train lumbers off, its rumble softens. Right now
I think of my life as complete. The envelope sealed.
I have nothing I want to return to. Nothing
that needs to be altered. I am burned clean, the boundaries
between me and this night erased. With my body
I hear each creak of pine, the murmur of stars
in the night sky, the soft clunk of wheels. Clean
as if before yet another beginning, a new birth
into something—I don't know what. But will there be
children, mothers, will a mother call me home
from where I sit in the garden now? Will there be
these very same pine trees? There is no way
I can go beyond what I have already known—
to develop a thirst for anything other
than pure bliss.

Everything
which made up that moment
stays there. No other here
and now. The evening, the path to the station,
the cloud of crows above the park, the squeezing
of two hands, the first shriek
of a train in motion. Not much remains,
not much at all. But enough so that years later
in a cold room I gnaw my fingers to the bone.
But I won't cry out, make a show of my feelings.
I'll only describe: an evening, the path, a cloud
of black crows and a train, everything
that was there at the time. The rest
doesn't exist. It's only a memory. Only
my memory. What happened inside
is not a fit subject for words.

I haven't forgotten a thing. And now
while the heat from the seventh summer
since that August shimmers above the asphalt,
I remember her name, her flustered look and my
bashfulness. Even today I can travel those roads
without missing a step. With no trouble
I make my way to that same stretch of blacktop
underneath the rowan trees. I remember
every detail. But it adds up
to only pain. Coming at us on a bicycle
an old farmer. He passes by, and for a second
his eyes look with attention
into mine. He is closer
to me than she is. He and I breathe
the same air, the same smell of new-mown hay,
the heat dancing on this road
baked in the sun, the sun which came up today
and then died. Everything
in my memory is lifeless. That attentive look
on the hot pavement, the stacks of fresh
pungent hay, the rowan trees weary
of their everlasting endurance
in the blaze of afternoon.

Pigeons asleep on the ledges and cornices
of the Sukiennica, trusting as children. Just
stick out your hand—the warm arousal and flutter,
the quick-beating heart. On the steps of the monument
young men and women cluster
around a guitar and sing. The damp blue darkness,
the orange light shining on the walls, purity
of evening and song. It hurts. To think
at first it was because of you
I fell in love with this city.

May, an unexpected downpour. People hole up
in a courtyard entrance. The sun still shines
through the rain. The air glows. The narrow passage
through Szewska Street is bathed in radiant
blue light. One of the moments you cannot lose
if you make this place your home. But don't
waste time thinking—stick your head out the door.
Let the cold drops stream down your cheeks
as you watch the young girl standing
a few steps away, her hair drenched, summer blouse
transparent from the rain, her radiant gaze
blushing when she notices you are looking. But try now
not to think about anything. Just feel
the fresh metallic dampness on your skin.
And don't turn away your eyes. Later,
it will only take a few drops of rain
to stream down your cheeks, for you
to conjure her up again.

Up all night, then daybreak. Time
to get out of the house. The fog, the sun
low on the horizon, the grass wet with dew,
the racket of the birds impossible to ignore,
the windows empty, dark. No one out
in the streets. The market empty.
Never before have I heard each step
so clear on the pavement. Never before
has my own heartbeat filled my ears
as I walked down the street, its nervous
rhythm, each moment more and more
irregular. Finally, in the Planty,
I meet the milkman pulling his cart,
broadcasting his wares. Now, I am able
to go back

Weighed down by his bags, gray whiskers on his chin,
he heads down the same path of the Planty
that you do, basking in this April day. But actually
he travels through some other weather, some other
place and time. His eyes filmed over, oblivious
to the world around him, he looks straight through you
to a world you will never see. The borders
which can never be crossed. Only when hungry, his hand
reaches back over the edge, accepting a coin
or roll left over breakfast. He is
from far away. But then again,
consider yourself. You are where he is.
Equally alone.

On a June day I open the window. The play
of light on the river, the river
which happens to be named the Vistula. Bridges,
towers whose green domes look like trees, trees
which look like green towers. There are sky blue
tramcars filled with people, their voices.
There are voices, all the voices
which ought to be here, everything which knows
the art of living. There is no other truth
than this. So don't be surprised, don't ask.
It is time to ripen, to be
like a child tottering on the verge
of a secret
openly revealed.

Evenings I walk the town, the lit streets,
the Market Square. Later, I work
on a new poem—almost every night.
As a poet before me said—this
is happiness. I don't know. All
I can do is describe the waves of people
on the Square, their noise and energetic heat,
how their cheeks swell up
with the air we share between us,
our upturned faces washed by each flake
of the fall of twilight, the darkness
steeped in the warmth of the human body,
the lamplight glancing off a woman's hair. So how
do I describe? The poet before me is silent
to this most simple question. His mouth
filled with dust. The dust
to which everything returns.

The sound of a bawling child through the walls each night,
the pacifying and bedside song. The tattered remains
of voices from other rooms:
"I don't know never mother I'm already coming
keep in mind why everything will turn out okay."
From behind my apartment wall, from behind
every wall that exists, the conversations
never die down. I can't see any faces or eyes.
But I hear what is said. Unbelievable
the ties that strap us together, that strap
each thing with each thing. No way
to filter out. No room
for a breath taken freely
and without fault.

If someday I must describe
these times, what will I say? About
what created me, my nagging unease and crazy desire
that this unease will never be abandoned. But maybe
I can say this more simply: I'll mention
the nightly tramps I made through the city, everything
I felt at the time. Someday the gift
of naming will come. Already understanding the meaning,
I will recall these last few days—the newspapers
voicing the latest triumphs of crime and madness, no one
realizing the stories pertain to them. Or maybe
I will select one single event—torn
out from the others, easy to catch because it is dead.
Perhaps better I keep silent. Mention only
how very, very much I was afraid
that a future would come when no one
would be by my side, would hear me
as I confided: "You know, don't you,
how in those days
I was very much afraid?"

Night, the mountains, a storm. The shelter packed with people.
A bright flash. As quick as the fall of a leaf the moment
of waiting for the thunder. How long? A few seconds. But what
is a second? An eon in a falling drop's history, the lifespan
of a bacterium, the time for two or three human breaths,
or maybe more, depending on the urgency of the moment. Fright,
agony, love. A few seconds, enough to fit in birth, death,
nothingness. So how to measure it?—All this I managed to think
before the thunder buckled down the mountain. The heavy
sigh of relief of everyone around the fire. Still it will all
come again. The painful interval between the flash and rumble,
a time for only a few thoughts, for only one life. One barely
has time to think—to recognize people's faces, nervous glances,
gripped knuckles and held breath. Just barely able,
looking at them, to realize we live in the frailest of eons.
The lightning already passed, the thunder yet to fall.
Only this moment—the last frail leaf
of time.

My imagination is so particular it sees the
tear drop, the smallest and crazy leaf in the maple's
shaky crown, a wrinkle on the face I loved
young and unspoiled. My imagination
is also banal, ready to take for the kernel of truth
what I look at now: a haphazard meeting
in some deserted alley, a boy and a squirrel
which creeps up slowly, cautiously, to his outstretched
beseeching hand, a squirrel urged on by hunger, oblivious
to the light in the boy's eyes, kindled now to a blaze
not even he as an adult will extinguish. My imagination
doesn't even reach the borders of the possible.
It does not dread the yellow or purple flash
which will burn up the sun, the spatter
of some sort of sticky substance, the sudden
burst of pain beneath the skull
which will end everything. It's all
a bunch of nothing. Nothing
besides a face that I loved. A maple tree. Nothing
besides the kernel fulfilling itself in
the communion between animal and man. No kernel
of truth at all. Nothing beyond
the imagining.

Glimpsed in passing from a train,
this foggy evening, the gray band of smoke
hanging motionless above the field, the wet
blackness of the earth, the sun
almost set. Faraway, on the fading disk
around me, are two small specks, two women
in dark head scarves, maybe returning from church. Maybe
one says something, tells some ordinary history,
maybe a sinful love—her words
so extraordinary and simple. But from them
the whole story gets created
from the very beginning. So remember this
and keep it with you forever. The sun, the plowed earth,
women, love, evening, these few words
good for any beginning. Remember—
tomorrow we are likely
to be somewhere else entirely.

A December evening full of noise, colorful lights.
On the Market Square music, voices. On my glove the small star
of a snowflake burns out. An entire world melting
into a froth of dirty water underneath my hot breath. My breath
fertile as it is destructive. I watch its white cloud
blossom from my mouth. The sign
I am alive. I watch the same clouds, the same sign of life,
come from the people's mouths around me. A pact
which we share between us.
                                        Late at night I take
the same path home. Underneath the fresh snow the Market
looks alien and cold. There is no one out. No trail
beaten through the snow. The squeak beneath my boots
is the only sign of life. My life, no one else's.
Then suddenly I feel it. Someone is looking
on this snowy star we call the earth, a star
surrounded by the warm cloud of human breath. And I know
for a moment he must be holding his breath. A moment—
the entire time we know.

Coming from their mouths, these words
are calm and strong. But only when the time has come
to say them. They will say no, they will say enough.
They will say the words disgrace and truth. These words
will not be comical or banal
when said by these tight-lipped men
who feel the need to speak up
at no other time. The women will listen in silence,
hands suddenly stopped in their work,
the children at that moment
will understand everything. And
that moment is now. There are silent women,
their arms helplessly lowered. There are children
who are no longer in the dark. There are words
which demand a mouth—when derision
is the only thing we hear.

Who will bear witness to these times. Who
will write down? For it won't be one of us.
We have lived here too long, absorbed
this age too deeply. We are too faithful
to speak the truth. To speak any truth at all. Faithful,
I say justice, and dwell on the dark happiness of revenge.
I say the word concern, but I think them versus us. I think
what they did to me. Nothing more
do I have in my defense: I was faithful, I was weak—
weak that I hated those of evil, weak that to protect truth
I used sleight of hand, weak that scorn was my own
diseased brand of pride. Hate, scorn, lies. So many years—
just to survive and stay clean. As if to survive
and stay clean is possible at all. But above all—to survive.
To remain—not speaking. But still to keep on asking
who will bear witness—knowing it won't be one of us.
Nor anyone. Not a single word. An empty age. But still
it pulsed with life like no other, because it was our life,
and there will never be a second one like it. Shriek, roar,
laughter, tears and howling, an old tune
without any words. Not a single word which one day
might be said on our behalf.

From *Family Album* (*Album rodzinny*) and *Extinction of the Holy City* (*Zagłada świętego miasta*)

Rain outside the window, on the table a glass of tea,
a lamp glowing. Naïve, but that's how I see you
in five, twenty, a hundred-twenty years as you read
this poem and think about me, from a generation
or a century ago. You wonder how it was
I lived. My life and times, the bottomless
weariness of people. A few names and dates, a few
fields of defeat, all the magic formulas
repeated with the childlike hope of the living,
lacking the wisdom time has given you
who live after us and everything we know. I have
so little to pass down, so little
just as everyone else. But I know
I lived and I don't want to be completely erased—
to become for you another statistic
for pity or scorn. What I was, what
could have been me and nothing else, remains
on the outside of history. And I can only speak
the language accessible to us both—the smell of rain
settling the dust of the city (yes,
it is raining here, too), the pain in my elbow
cracking the edge of the table, the ticking clock,
the taste of hot tea, and the light, glaring in my eyes,
as I write this poem in the common language
of our five
immortal senses.

A September afternoon, I inhale
the scent of the sun-baked firs, listen
to the roar of the Białka as I squint
at the dazzle of its white foam,
the whiteness of sun and water. I breathe,
listen, watch. There is nothing else. But then
I think of everything I escaped from
to reach this one pure moment of happiness, one
impossible moment. Maybe someone, years from now,
in this same place, same afternoon,
will do it for me, someone
just like me, maybe even my son, his pureness
of pleasure and thought. Sometime: the blighted hope
of the people of this age.

Through the weight of this uneasy summer's air, the noise
of this fretful city, she walks—wearing a loose skirt
and light blouse, the same thing so many girls
this year are wearing. But this is what makes
her different. She looks not seeing
that we are watching. Our glances can't touch
her proud white forehead, held upright, her brisk
unhurried steps. She is separate, unfathomable, a cool
patch of rain on a stuffy, crowded street. Immaculate,
unblemished. But somewhere in this city, someone
must know her tears, her weariness, her proud
white breasts,
unclothed.

No one will ever claim the age we live in. We
will remain stray and homeless. No pain or compassion,
only the ache of shame and fear
that what we saw might come again. The need to forget
and erase from the page. "An exception to the rule,"
I will say of those who can talk in such terms
of a life unrepeatably human, their urge to destroy
the evidence most damaging of all—our small
personal mementos, dangerous because
they are raw and spontaneous. A couple, their child
asleep, takes one last look at a photo
of a young man and woman with light blond hair
surrounded by the honey thickness
of a July afternoon, the air rich with insects
and the smell of mown grass. The young man and woman
gaze back at the lens, curious and thirsty, on the porch
of an old house shaded by red pines. This house, these trees,
stand till today, the one last witness that this
was how it once was. No wonder
that the couple will panic. They rub from the photo
her face, my face, both our faces, hoping
that this will prevent
the same thing from happening
to them.

One of the last leaves to break loose from the maple
twirls in the clean October air, joins its fellows,
and dies. No one was there to see
its battle with the wind, no one was there to follow
its flight. No one would be able
to come along and pick it out from the other leaves heaped
on the pile. No one saw it
but me. No one. I
was alone.

Not at once did you grasp the message. The evening
after long hours on the beach. Alone, alert,
you let nothing escape. The majesty of the last
moments of the sun, the waves lit by fire and pearl, the clouds
like dancing glaciers and the tide's unexhausted roar.
The everlasting miracle of the sunset. And you, dazzled,
recognized. Then you headed back
through the warm murk of the pine forest, the sudden silence
and shadow, the sandy path, and finally a road and lights.
It was then you saw: in front of a tourist cabin,
on a bench, an old man (who could have been your father)
swayed back and forth, tapping his foot as he played
an easy tune on the harmonica. Before him a little boy
(who could have been your son), in a billed cap,
jumped and danced, singing off-key. At that moment nothing
connected these two moments—the incoming surge of the elements
and this simple human joy—
but you. You saw these parts one right after the other.
And only you could fill the space
between grandfather and grandson, enter in the midst
of their unknown names. All this you thought
you had grasped right then. But it is only now, later,
that you truly become dazzled, to see the old man and boy
in a new light, as you hear once again the everlasting psalm
that comes from the simple majesty of their lips. They
are the true messengers
of a jealous God, who demands
to be recognized
in the meekest of his creatures, those he made
like you, in his own image.

Evening, the Kraków train station, three gypsy
children beg. With the grace of young animals,
agile and joyful, they whirl through the crowd,
disappearing, calling out to each other
in their unfathomable tongue. Nothing links them to you,
except for a moment, the warmth of a coin you press
quickly and shamefully to the palm
of this fourteen-year-old girl, proud and self-assured,
her indulgent smile and steady gaze
older than you or memory, the unnerving touch
of a separate reality. Then she runs off
and you watch the leap of her ponytail,
her scarf and bare heels. The cold marble stairs
she touches are different, the crowd of people
around her she sees in a different way. She hears
the voice over the loudspeaker,
not knowing a word it says, not knowing
how freely she can breathe, how easily
she can cancel and discard your whole world.
Later, the children, off to the side,
raucously split up their booty. The oldest yells
and they vanish. You remain, and suddenly
you feel the breath-taking urge—to run like them,
barefoot in the cold and damp, to whirl
in this alien, barren world, and then return home
calling "I'm coming! I'm coming!"
in a language no one else can understand,
the gleeful child
of an unknown God.

Meager landscapes of childhood, just a few places, not the most
holy. A drowsy summer camp outside of Łódź, the Gorce Mountains, the
limestone cliffs looking on Jasna Góra. You had no choice. And
no revocation. When you think of mountains, or dream them, you can see
nothing more. Gentle wooded ridges and the black silhouette of Luboń Hill,
the Grabia—drowsy beneath the alders—that shall always be The River,
while the sun on the dark towers of Częstochowa will be the only form
of light ever given unto you. All this has passed and yet
you remain. Disinherited from the world's holy brilliance, imprisoned
in what you were at the time—sentenced. But you are here. Go
to the window, spread your arms and look—further, further. Free
it all up. Allow nothing to stop. Yes, the world. Forgive and fulfill.
In every river, that one drowsy drop of water, green from the alder
trees. And, shining from the monastery cliffs, the one
light that without cease will wrest away the darkness and set up
the brilliant white towers
of all Eternal Cities.

Your train arrive? You're here? That's good. No matter where you go,
like now, awakened in a hotel in the heart of the City of Light,
you will return: the needle-strewn path from the garden gate;
the pine trees' shade; the patio with its cracked tile; the damp, cool
walls of this house. Jolka, Małgosia, Jarek, Ela, Auntie—
just like then and henceforth—steeped with their life, even if not all
are still living—death does not possess such power. And one
of their number, you—the city of light extinguished by a dark puff of wind—
make it to them, just like in that dream a moment ago,
evening, already from the gate you see their outlines
in the window you listen—because death does possess this power—
already from the patio you hear the laughter and that voice—no other
will do, you refuse it, you plead—as it emerges from the lips
of your Uncle Jasia: Your train arrive? You're here? That's good.

Lazy summer afternoon, clouds of mosquitoes near the river,
sweet flag, cool greenness of the water, the avenues of willows
along the Wkra, the village organist in a carefully buttoned
down frock coat returns home from choir practice. His first child,
a young girl, already waits by the gate. He quickens his step,
so much still before him: six sons, building a house, a quarrel
over a field, a dress ball, a sleigh ride and a journey
in a closed train car to the final station, a small town
in Southern Poland named Auschwitz. . . . For the thousandth time
this other man checks in the mirror for the traces, always painful,
of the Cossack's sword, then puts away the mirror, takes a look
at the sharp towers of Częstochowa, the cliffs of Castle Heights,
while nearby through the garden a small breathless boy
gallops up on a stick horse, his son—while at the sudden
recollection of that cavalry charge the man touches his scar
and is soothed: I'm alive. Then he opens the window wide.
Lazy afternoon, between the pines the glint of sunshine.
Sunshine, coolness of water, sweet flag, willow and pine—
it all exists, both solid and intertwined.—To be sure
they never did meet—my father's father and the father
of my mother. They knew nothing of each other. Only the world
can unite them—unite them with me. I can see them enclosed
by the air living at that moment. It could have been that way
and so it was.—And is. This summer afternoon and the question
of what I am to them. I, who have seen Częstochowa's towers
pierce through the clouds of dust, and the glint of the Wkra
as it gives off steam.

Life swells to twice, three times its normal size,
your heart fluttering in your throat, joy, unease and joy,
as if before a great ball like yesterday's. The candles,
mirrors, the waxed dance floor—it all swirls around you,
Joasia in her long white dress, her eyes as she presents you
with her ribbon, the songs around the piano, the hugs
of mustached old men, exaltation, and then a few hours'
sleep echoing with music. Now, morning, before the porch,
so much clean air, space, the sun on snow, the warm smell
of chimney smoke, your hand on your heart, there—
underneath your cloak—her ribbon. She looks on. She knows
where it is and is flustered. So many voices,
someone's wailing once again you listen
to the holiest of words, the whining of dogs, they jump up
on your knees, your chest. Before the cry to mount, Jan,
lord of the manor, kisses your shoulder, then on
through the village, black shapes outlined in white,
someone making the sign of the cross, the snow
squeaking underfoot, your slow gait, and then faster,
the January air in your lungs, the ferocious snorts
of the horses, faster, through the row of poplars, the rattle
of riding gear, the sound of guns, and still
there is so much green hope
in this act of dying.

I see a gray house amongst pines red with the sunset.
On the porch, my grandfather, his back up against a post,
says something to a reddish cat he calls Maciej. The cool
air filled with the scent and creaking of the pines, this house
an old man, a cat, this evening—its breath surrounding me—
none of this could ever exist together, it only meets
here in my imagination for the blink of an eye, its single
total existence. I think these things up, surround them
with shared air, fill them with life. But in the blink of an eye
the toil of imagination stops, the lucidity of thought—
everyone and everything that has ever been without cease,
without blinking—also slowly comes to lose
both power and light, the bone-wearied thought
that finally collapses: this is the way we see—and this
our one and only world—in darkness, in uproar, in madness.

It takes but a few moments. Foggy morning, largest market square
of the old Europe, the voices of the city still uncertain. Then.
Fire, blinding yellow, horror and paralysis. In the bank's
doorway the changing in dollars and vodka stops, the wings
of the crowd flitting around the man who—having chained himself
to the Old Town pump—is burning. The smell of gas, instantaneous.
His clothes and then hair. The spasm of hands and mouth. Voice,
distorted by pain, becomes just a scream, no longer managing
to form words, the caustic brown smoke of the refused sacrifice
not rising to the skies, not stopping in a sign. Instead
it just crawls, close to the ground, disappears, until absorbed
by the lungs of the crowd which, just a few seconds later,
retakes up life. Once again, in the doors across the way,
they start to change dollars and vodka, the crowd
starts slowly winging out, away, the last flame
of the old Europe expiring as the city in victory proclaims: How, burning,
   can you ever
know freedom? Everything yours,
betrayed.*

* Translator's Note: This poem describes the self-immolation of Walenty Badylak
on March 21, 1980, in protest of the Communist Regime's ongoing suppression of
any recognition of the Katyń massacre of nearly 22,000 Polish army officers by the
Soviet Army during World War II. Badylak, a member of the Polish Home Army
during the war, had previously been a baker by trade, but his bakery had been
closed down by the authorities because of his activism.

The world: full and indivisible, starts here at the end
of my hands. Standing by the window, I can see it: the green
towers of Skałka and Wawel, the dome of St. Ann, farther on the hills
dark blue, because the woods look this way towards evening, behind them
valleys, filled up with cities, and then more cities still:
on rivers, in the sprawling plains, descending to the sea, beyond which
there is still another sea, sharp brown peaks, passes,
roads, people's homes no different from
my own. The breath filling up my mouth, my lungs and blood,
just a ration—mine for just a while—of the full arc of air
wrapping around the earth, indivisible. I see it—I know
it is there—at arm's length—at hand, this warmth of breath,
the rest just a reading of kilometers, a deficiency of sight—trivial
on the scale of mind and heart. Thus
at arm's length, a few streets away, in a great square
filled up with people, my brother takes aim
and shoots my father. Here, at hand.
This way. Not with a whimper or a bang. This way.*

May 13, 1981

* Translator's Note: On May 13, 1981, the Polish-born Pope John-Paul II (Karol Wojtyła) was shot and nearly killed in Rome by a Turkish gunman, Mehmet Ali Agca, a member of the militant right wing group Grey Wolves. The attack sent a shock wave of worry throughout Poland. A couple of years later, Pope John-Paul met with Agca, who had been sentenced to life in prison, and reported afterwards: "What we talked about will have to remain a secret between him and me. I spoke to him as a brother whom I have pardoned and who has my complete trust."

This city died. Blue tram cars grate
on the curves. The nervous gray crowd not fitting
inside the streets, bright lights bleached from neons. Voices,
dust and fumes. This city dead from the time you realized
how easy it could die. And they are wrong, those
who think it will arrive in flashes, in a great thunderclap
according to the spirit of the Word, or the Bard snickering it
will arrive on cat's feet. They are all wrong
as to method. And they are not prepared. In mid-word
of an unsent letter, of a woman's unfulfilled love, of a sin
turned mortal because never is divulged. No one
will be ready. Yet, you must love what is doomed: there
is no other love. To say goodbye as if forever, this is
to be forgiving and kind. To not put off for the morrow,
not stifle those words both weighty and vast. There might
not remain any more time, any more room. From now on
there will be no other love. This city
is everywhere.

Maybe it will happen in the span of a sentence, between
the first and last word of the poem. A poem
about freedom—for no matter who might be speaking, a poet
always speaks of their freedom. They speak of the women
and the men of *their* time, of the light in the mountains,
of the breath of the nighttime sky, of white and pink apple trees, *going*
through a village, of the children by the well, the impatience of the heart,
the clamor of cities, the pure sound of the trumpet in the tower, about God
   and the delight
of the body. They speak of solitude and become no longer alone, they speak
about their times and shall *always* take from it: the people
of one's city, the longings of children, *trees* bearing forth, voices,
the lights and the hills, and they take also from death: the *entire* cosmos
in a drop of rain *glistening* outside *the window*, colors, the slang
of a Sunday street, the *quiet* falling snow. All of them exists. Their speech
is their blood, their body, their soul. Freedom. And the named world
from this point will hold *only one* time: It is. It is
right there between the first and *last word* of this poem—
this one you are reading. Yes, *maybe it will happen*
between the first and last word of this very poem,
between the first and last word
about freedom. *

* Translator's Note: In the original Polish, all italicized words and passages are in Lati-
nized Russian, suggestive of the Russian language infiltrating and then supplanting
the native Polish. More information about this poem is available in the introduction.

The valley flooded with sunlight among the hills
overgrown with a lush black and green forest. Summer heat,
in the honey-like air swarms of small flies vibrate, the
perk and drone of bees, the heads of grass nodding
laden with seed, the thistle-tops swaying. Two martins
skim the meadow's surface, in the sky a squall of starlings,
a swallowtail butterfly drowses, purple, on a milkweed pod.
Hot breath of earth, penetrating smell of mint and mud lily
clogging up the bed of the still distinct river. Yellowish
molehills, on the slope a thicket of blackberries, dark
juices stirring in the fruit, warming from the sun,
the fullness: the dance of dragonflies, the euphoria
of insects—and, describing a perfect circle, a buzzard,
serene and ceremonious, gazes for its prey: suspended
above the waves of fen and bog, and from out
of the bottom of the valley, as the everlasting sign
of the rhyme and reason, the four corners
of the earth—they go out: on the west
Szewska Street, Floriańska on the north.
To the west Mikołajska,
And Grodzka to the south.*

* Translator's Note: The four streets at the end of the poem are the four main
streets leading out from the Market Square of Kraków's Old Town.

From *Weariness* (*Zmęczenie*)

This Day

Rapture of breath, gift of memory,
birthright of hunger, sleep and desire,
miracle of sight and ongoing blessing
of the skin with its pain and pleasure. Who
can take it? O Lord, for one second I beg you
forget I am your creature.

Some Other Language

My fourteenth autumn in Kraków. The city
has slowly stripped itself of color, dressed
in a single layer of grime. Instead of air,
always fog, and in the fog, someone speaks to me—
perhaps in Polish. I can make out
words, but I don't understand the sense.
It has already crumbled. Maybe
it's because he is speaking some other language
that has already gone extinct.

All Souls

Fourteen years in one place. Long enough to have several
Graves to visit: Ela, Piotr, Leszek, Janusz, Staszek,
Gwizdek. All of them younger than I. Already
I feel no pain when I look at their lives. They are free
of sharp edges, perfect and complete
as fruit ready on the limb. So beautiful,
so unobtainable, for those of us who
in our clumsy and chaotic way
still fiddle with the day to day business
of how we die.

This Age

The same age as Christ, the age
of defeat. Any idea
of what I want? No,
I only know what I don't want—
to die. At least not
to go on dying like this.

Distance

What does it mean when two men breathe
the same smell of decaying leaves, regard
the same stark tree? Little.
I watch. He watches. The tree
keeps dying. We stand here
side by side The distance we share
between us.

Without Pathos or Metaphysics

All things give up the stage. From the Old Market Square
I go up Szpitalna Street. Anesthetized workers,
drinking since dawn, demolish a townhouse built
when Poland still existed. Powder from the bricks
turns into mud. It's December,
Tuesday. Just a few more days
till Christmas Eve.

After All the Roar and Thunder and Toil

Housing development. The cement and claustrophobic mountains
of apartment buildings drowned inside the night. They sleep—
the silent, the murky, the small—the disinherited
of the kingdom of the earth. They sleep. Disinherited now
even of their own name, their own face and memory. Unowned
these blinded heirs of light—incited to rise up and topple
over on their backs, helpless. They sleep, while waking around them
are demons, a pack of wild dreams, ravenous
nothingness. Clairvoyant, invisible, unsatiated
moths—flocking off
to darkness.*

* Translator's Note: The title is taken from a very short—and rather disillu-
sioned—poem written in 1833 by Adam Mickiewicz, perhaps the greatest of
Poland's Romantic poets. A visionary of national independence, he spent a good
part of his life in exile, and died of cholera during a journey to Constantinople to
aid Polish soldiers fighting against Russia in the Crimean War. Mickiewicz's poem
is thus a kind of oracular warning of what might happen, while the poem above
describes the situation as already coming to pass. Here is a rough translation of the
Mickiewicz poem:

Mouths Shouting Out in the People's Name

Mouths shouting in the name of the people will one day bore the people.
Poses struck in the name of the people will one day tire the people as well.
Hands that fight in the name of the people the people will one day cut off.
Those names now beloved by the people the people will forget.
Everything passes. After all the roar and thunder and toil,
To inherit the earth will be the silent, the murky, the small.

Weariness

So, at last it will come to rest, to drowse off and sleep
on your heart. You feel the weak and winded breath
of Europe, so slight, so helpless, you can
take it in your clasped hands, like a fledgling. You
lift your hands higher, and it will take wing. Spirit
above the waters.

Not Again

It was only a second. Now, once again among
the living, I swear to never
repeat that inhuman prayer. "Throw out
these rotting eggs, these dog-eared
figures on display, breathe out fire, cleanse,
open up the door and lead us. We, O Lord,
are ready."

From *Light* (Światło)

First Sight

Daybreak. I open my eyes. I open
myself. Once again I have returned intact and take up
the world and the light anew. I might not see
the contours of the room, the willow outside my window,
the fact of the Absent. Not one scrap of sky, not one
thing at all. But I see the light and the light all around
looks back at me. I am—
because of light.

Allow This

Allow this, bounteous and blessed with being: for the wind
to run through your veins and lungs: for the unseeing
light to glimpse
the world with your own eyes—
allow this: to take up dwelling with you
the God
disowned from his own house.

Star, Droplet

This dark star, this droplet of blood, this one tear,
one drop of the universe poised and quivering
before falling down. On the fields and plazas and valleys,
swelling the rivers and the eyes. This star, this drop,
this second in which your fate
rose up and fell apart.

Sleep, Snow

Sleep, now—soft and warm spiral downward,
the black flakes of ash, falling so slowly
in the silence, covering so carefully and delicately
all the earth, the houses and streets. So sleep, sleep
in peace, in safety: the cities, the houses, the gardens,
the eyes and the ears, safe. Nothing bad
can ever happen. Everything has
already taken place.

Summer, in the Distance

Lightning, in a calm, clear sky, far
away, silent. So far away, somewhere or other, the sound
does not reach us. Not to us the fire speaks
as it snatches up hayracks and standing fields, enters
the bunched sheaves of houses not our own. Above
whose heads does it now cry out—still not speaking
a language we can know—air, war, famine, the sharp
lash of fire. Above whose head
a Crown of Lead. Nothingness
and smoke.

At Night, on a Bench in Front of the House

In the stillness, the warm breath of the garden, I gaze at a star
which in this same moment
looks so shelterless, so betrayed and hungry, led
off to death. So now who is left
to forgive me?

The Light

That kind of time. Chaos has won and darkness
covers the earth
and the sky, and in between them——me. Still
I keep fighting, still
I keep breathing: I defeat the chaos
and the darkness inside. On earth
and in heaven. Right here
between us.

A Petition

After forty nights and forty nights
recede the dark, hungry waters of commotion.
After a great weeping as if a great storm—allow me
to rise up and go. Far, far away. Not one thing
carried with me, without memory. Clean. Underneath
a new name, underneath new clouds, and in
my own new body, clean. "Light, light, light
of the world bear me along with your blood, and the words
of speech which no one has used—-they await
my arrival." In the vast stillness that follows
such a great weeping. In the stillness, without words,
but with the immaculate voices of earth,
of water, of air—speak unto me, touch me and stir
me to life.

At Night, Returning in Rain

Rain: eternal, spreading without end.
O home, awaiting my return—envelop
and soak down inside me, make me
become you once again. Reconcile.

Totentanz

How much rapture, and how pure. It is the light, it
is the air, it is the life of this moment. It is. We hold
each other by the hand; we walk and run. Dear Ania
with her armful of herbs and grasses; the glint of eyes
so warm and happy; smack down the middle of Szewska
Street; Uncle Benedict in the Planty Gardens
tossing his umbrella along with all caution; pigeons
scattered with a laugh; Gwizdek without stammering unburdens
himself to his professor; Mirek with a letter from The Master,
brash and proud; Marek Teodor with his everlasting hat; and then
like the glistening surface of a lake, opening up
the Old Market Square, sprinkled lightly, just on the surface,
by a sunlit rain; Grandma in a brand new white dress from the end
of the last century; the warm gaze of naked skin; the dark
odor of hair; and all around the Cloth Hall, Adam's bass voice
roars up a storm like a bumblebee suspended in a meadow; a chain
of hands, and the procession—but who is leading?—passes. On
through the flowerstalls as if into a throbbing
overwhelming garden, accelerated breaths, voices, hands,
so many warm hands, so much rapture—that we know, for certain,
any moment now, He will come and speak to us: here
in the last second of chaos
before His first Word.

An Excerpt

Watch, o helpless death. More and more they are made flesh—
men and women, rivers, streets, mountains, rain and grass,
moments and clouds. They negate you, o nothingness. Surrender,
open up, turn to our side, beautiful and unbounded, sing
in the choir that gives its praises
to life. . .

In June

The cemetery on Salwator—lush island
of old trees—sails off in the wind, glistening. The green
mirror of the sky, the noisy kindergarten
of birds, but not even a little leaf,
O Death, for you.

Rapture

Daylight, a chorus—the slow plying boats
of clouds, the unsung song
of light. Where to?
Will you lead? O my Radiant
Guide.

Genesis

From the mist emerges the world—obscure, unspoken,
unnamed. An early November snow falls on the still green grass,
the white snowdrifts of reflected light, clustered sparklings in the trees,
where the Vistula bends beneath Wawel Castle the flock of mute swans
that winter here every year, while on the Dębnicki Bridge the unruly
din of the city, the disk of the setting sun. Unclear and unnamed
the day disappears. Just then a man and woman draw near, different among
so many walking the river's edge—lovers. For the first time
they hold each other's hand, for the first time together
they see the unnamed flotillas of clouds, the unspoken
syllables of waves, the vowels of the world and the light—obscure,
muted, mortal. And all is brought to life. And
to offer it to her, the man starts to give names
to all the visible world, while from this day forward exist only
those things that could ever be. The man stretches out his hand and
says bridge, river, sun, snow, grass, tree, God, swaddled child
who, unknowingly imitating the movement of human lips
learns—once again—
to speak.

From *Such Freedom (Taka wolność)*

No One, Everyone

Who wants to hear my version—
love, hate, the unfinished miracle
of the world? No one. November,
the wind, bare-boned, callous,
vexes the city's sleep. When its
voice rises,
everyone stops to listen.

Song to a Flake of Snow

But if this be Your sign and mercy,
This clean snow is of no avail:
Each flake like an angel sent down
To degradation and death

In mid-flight the sight of earth attracts it like a mirror:
As soon as it falls it no longer is a star
Dying on my forehead a host of tiny mouths
Baby kisses of hot burning iron

Vigilia, Christmas Eve

Empty street. Mercury quivers in the lamps.
The crunch on the shiny grit of snow.
No one to accost you, not even the wind
Grabs you by the sleeve.

The warm silent caves of windows
Cast on the snow their fat yellow light.
So splash on through it. It's all you can do.
No one will grab your coat sleeve from behind.

And learn to love these dirty prisms of packed snow.
The cold bead of water streaming down your face:
Where to run to?
Where to run to?
Where to run to?

I am weary
but cannot bring myself to sleep
cannot spit out the taste of this day:
I've breathed in their air
spoken with their words
traveled using their streets—
weariness
the eye aching in the glow from the lamp
the shadow of my head
on the paper with this poem:
these things of mine
I have managed to rescue

Evening the empty fields smelling of earth
dew settling in on the tops of my boots
dogs barking from the village faraway the first light
no one to speak to me
no one to count my footsteps no one to wait for me
for no one
does my absence even register
beneath this darkening bare sky
such freedom

I know that somewhere
is the purest spring
and too much I desire
that this spring not be the one
from which I will wash myself
of everything I am—
that I not be disappointed
by my iron ration of the air
or this little morsel of hysteria
always nudging me towards the light—
just this little chain
of heartbeats
counting out quietly the sounds of my poems
that will not even last—to break myself free
and then go.

My hands touch the surfaces
of so many other objects—of hands warm skin a cat
my sight moves past the walls the faces the lights
without a sound or trace
my lips give form
to words so many words—
but I am already absent
this road is unknown
but out in the open I can breathe

This much can be confirmed:
from nearby it's so clear
the gray wrinkled skin
the tremor in the left corner of the mouth
of the eye
the tired face of the woman
who gave me birth—
a word or two from her
a word or two from me
and then our silence

Chile

Chile

I

1

They harbor no ideas. In the words
among which they were born they are unable
to utter any human idea. Like animals stricken
from fright, they are not even cynical. Their insanity,
cowardice and servility make up
the laws of this country.

2

Their money, power and privilege
are motives for spreading death. If you
are to resist the weighing of human life
as if it were meat, you must never
close the book, the record
of what they have done. As long as you
remember, your own life will be worth more
than their money, power, and privilege, can buy.

3

They are the walking dead. That
is their sentence. The turncoats, thugs,
murderers. Dead. For them no room
in the hearts of the living. So many mouths
cursing their birth.

4

Each one a million times smaller than the evil
they do together. Each one a blind and blunt instrument
in the hands of another hired soul—himself
just a tool as well. They are what they perform—
nothing more. The unknowing, sightless pawns
of the Lord
of Darkness.

5

That which conquers me, becomes me. Even
while dying, collapsing beneath an unstoppable power
independent and harsh, I take on a part of it—
the part needed to defeat me. Dying, but not debased,
I grow. But conquered through weakness, baseness,
treachery, I am only to be pitied. The dupe
of cowardice and second-hand authority, Poland
can expect nothing more. It lives on,
the booty of petty thieves. No tragedy:
No need for great gestures.

II

1

You live in the same age I do. Your life is as precious
as mine. You breathe the same way. You have the same gift
of the senses. To express the pain, to give names to bread,
a child, the cross—you use the same words. Our blood
shares the same color. This is our birthright. But you
have discarded it, covering the emptiness
with a uniform. Soon nothing will remain but the lining
inside a government-issue coat.

2

Your hand forced the river to a standstill, changed it
into an unresponsive slough, filled the springwaters in
with a shovel. But for how long? Forever? Ridiculous.
We will still outlast you. You are just a small detail
thrown into the dawn, a moment swallowed by the day
the spring once again flows with the pulse of the earth. . .

3

When in scorn you say that your truth is a tank
and mine a butterfly, unknowingly you have said
a mouthful. As if through you
spoke the voice which breathes truth
into everything. You. Me. Or the butterflies
repeating themselves forever.

4

We desired the same thing. Happiness. Each
understanding it in his own way. But my happiness
will never be cause for your humiliation, enslavement,
death. There is a greater chasm between us
than between insect and stone—which after all do not try
to deprive each other of the world.

5

Don't fire at me. Say something
instead. Is it really true
that for your arguments
there are no words in the Polish language?

III

1

It's strange. Sometimes we think fascists don't spring
claws or fangs, their faces don't turn scarlet.
They only differ from us slightly. Just the fear and madness
crammed into them without relief. Nothing more. As if
in a moment of weakness, a waver of attention in the heart,
you too would bend to their side.

2

Hard to believe that the sun, earth's orbit, light,
nativity and growth—all would switch over
to the side of death. But for you, it's easy.
In your eyes the world no longer changes
its color and shape. To a slave
each season is the same.

3

It's beyond us. The way the words from a prayer,
from other people, from newspapers and our dreams
unite into a testimony we
are too weak to give. "O Lord, I am not worthy
of such a death. Come take this cup
from me."

4

Don't expect justice or compensation. At best
you will wreak revenge on some traitor or underling.
You will hurt someone in the name of truth, someone
who true to his age has no idea
of what the truth is.

5

Days, years, we breathe lies. So how to tell
good from evil, our words deprived of their shape,
their weight, their power to judge? As happens in the grip
of a deep dream, we are speechless. We call out desperately
for help, for a glimpse, for a shadow of understanding.
No one can hear us. But tomorrow, in a few years, our fate
will be repeated, faithful to the last word.

IV

1

Nothing shattered beyond repair. Truth stays the same
old truth. Untruth the same old tool in the hands
of the murderer. Just one more shadow added
to the color of our suffering. All this
to emphasize your challenge. Here is your place, your duty.
With us, O Poet, as always.

2

I am a poet. I always wonder
if this has meaning. Will I ever help you to escape
your bonds, to conquer your weakness and fear, to muster
the steadfastness of heart to resist humiliation? Am I vain
to think I can lead you to a safe place, or rescue
someone, not even you, but after you, by recording your bravery,
your steadfastness of heart, how far you managed to climb?

3

Help me. For I'm weak. Each day
I lose more faith and clarity of vision. Madness
sticks its fingers in me, the edge

of ultimate despair. Help me. There is no one
left for you to count on. No one
but me.

V

1

Only by doing nothing will you not do evil. The czar
and his henchmen control your every move. They will take
your purest, unintended act—and turn it
to their own purpose. Therefore do nothing. Forbid
your heart to even beat. Each stroke bears you
out from the calm, collected shore
of death.

2

You can't do much, but at least you can't live
as if nothing has happened. You can slip
your hand from theirs. It seems trivial.
But an important moment. The beginning
that will lead to their end.

3

Not even the most sensitive, the most sensible
will be able to separate our words from deeds, victims
from torturers. In the uproar, all sense of desire, decision,
work will be lost. All faces, names, equally strange.
Only misunderstanding, pity, laughter. While what is left
of our world bears witness anonymously. Words, deeds,
victims, torturers, each cancelled out by the other. Work
so that this not be the final account.

4

Carefully, but without fear, go
between the police cordons. In tiredness and doubt, go
amidst the triumph of this imperium of thugs, amidst
the false pity of the world. Go, on your shoulders
truth, generation to generation.

5

What will happen when you give him your hand? Which
is stronger? Love or crime? Will the blood on his hands
steam from the touch of your fingers? Will your fingers
become tainted, O Holy Father,
when you meet Our General?

VI

1

I can be killed, forced into resignation, even
into the service of these hired thugs. But I will never
be convinced. My lungs still expand, my blood
throbs with oxygen, my heart beats on. I feel hunger,
fatigue. I react to light and touch. I will never
be converted from my humanity.

2

Sirens, the pulsations of purple light, the long column
of trucks and armored cars cuts the city into two. We hang
on opposite walls of the cleft. But suddenly the chasm
seals up like the surface of water behind a boat. Death
is impotent. Our lives drown it out. Even now, as its blade,
the head of the column, reaches its final destination.
Yes, now, even as we speak.

3

Not even knowing your own importance, O swallow,
flitting above the bricks of the square from which only yesterday
they managed to scrub off the stains of blood. Right now
we need you so much that only God
could have been the one to create you.

4

Just because he is and is capable of singing.
Just because there is a tree, the morning, a clear sky.
He has no use for our hopes, our belief. He doesn't
weigh out our chances. He is and therefore he sings.
You
should try to be like him.

5

Don't mind the pain or desperation.
Don't stop, o mortally tired, overworked
heart. Keep beating. As long as we are left
to hear you.

Krakow, 1982–1983

Acknowledgments

Beloit Poetry Journal: "Coming from their mouths, these words. . .", "A December evening full of noise. . .", "Evening, a burning campfire, the outgoing rings. . .", "Evenings I walk the town. . .", "Everything. . .", "Glimpsed in passing from a train. . .", "If someday I must describe. . .", "May, an unexpected downpour. . .", "The sound of a bawling child through the walls each night. . .", and "Strange evening, I sit in the garden. . ."

Boulevard: "In June" and "Star, Droplet"

Central Park: "Chile," (nominated for a Pushcart Prize)

Chariton Review: "Night, the mountains, a storm. . ." "Not at once. . .", "Through the weight of this uneasy summer's air. . .", "Weighed down by his bags. . .", "Whenever he described to me this park. . .", and "Who will bear witness to these times. . ."

Crosscurrents: "Is it right of me to keep rummaging. . ."

Field: Contemporary Poetry and Poetics: "I see a gray house amongst trees red with the sunset. . .", "Lazy summer afternoon, clouds of mosquitoes near the river. . .", "My imagination is so particular. . .", "The valley flooded with sunlight among the hills. . .", and "Your train arrive? You're here? That's good. . ."

Graham House Review: "No one will ever claim the age we live in . . ." and "Probably he can only see. . ."

Green Mountains Review: "Summer, in the Distance" and "Totentanz"

Hawai'i Review: "All Souls"

International Poetry Review: "First Sight," "A Petition," "Vigilia, Christmas Eve"

Jelly Bucket: "Allow This," "At Night, On a Bench in Front of the House," "I know that somewhere. . .", "My hands touch the surface. . .", and "So much that can be confirmed"

Manhattan Review: "Evening, the Krakow train station. . .", "Life swells to twice, three times its normal size. . .", "On her way out this morning. . .", "One of the last leaves to break loose from the maple...", and "A September afternoon, I inhale. . ."

Marlboro Review: "After All the Roar and Toil and Thunder" and "Weariness"

North American Review: "Song to a Flake of Snow"

Paintbrush: "Another Language" and "This Age"

Plume: "Maybe it will happen in the span of a sentence. . ."

Salmagundi: "The train station at night. . ."

Seneca Review: "Quiet apartment in which someone lies dying. . .", "Why is it that in my world. . .", and "The world is a still life. . ."

Sonora Review: "In June" and "Stones, Wings"

Stone Country: "A dragonfly pinned to the trail. . ." and "Up all night, then day-break. . ."

Webster Review: "Distance," "No One, Everyone," "Not Again," "This Day," and "Without Pathos or Metaphysics"

"Evening, Coming Down from Salwator Hill," "An Excerpt," "Genesis," "It takes but a few moments. . .", "Meager landscapes of childhood. . .", "Sleep, Snow," "This city died. . .", and "The world: full and indivisible. . .", all appeared in *Here at the End of My Hands*, Translation Chapbook No. 37, in *MidAmerican Review*

The following poems also have appeared in these anthologies:

"An afternoon in August. . ." and "Rain outside the window. . ." in *Shifting Borders: East European Poetries of the Eighties* (Associated University Presses, Walter Cummins, ed.)

"I lie in the meadows, my face. . ." and "Pigeons asleep on the ledges and cornices. . ." in *Literary Olympians 1992* (Ford-Brown, Elizabeth Bartlett, ed.)

"I haven't forgotten a thing. . ." in *Men & Women: Together & Apart* (The Spirit That Moves Us Press, Morty Sklar and Mary Biggs, eds.)

"I will never write a long poem. . .", "Is it right of me to keep rummaging. . .", and "On a June day I open the window. . ." in *Literary Olympians II* (Crosscurrents, Elizabeth Bartlett, ed.)

I would also like to thank the following agencies for their financial and institutional support: the Fulbright U.S. Student Program; the Indiana University Polish Studies Center and its University of Warsaw counterpart, Ośrodek Studiów Amerykańskich; The College of Wooster, including the Henry Luce III Fund for Distinguished Scholarship and its Faculty Development Fund; and the Ohio Arts Council Individual Excellence Fellowship for Poetry. I would also like to extend personal thanks especially to Aleksander and Barbara Fiut, Jerzy Iłłg (and Wydawnictwo Znak), Karen Kovacik, Piotr Florczyk, William Heyen, Derek Mong, Leonard Kress, Mania Dajnak, Urszula Kożiół (who introduced me to Bronisław Maj and his poetry), and to Margaret Meeker-Bourne, whose wise counsel has extended from punctuation choices to how to keep the books in my backpack balanced as we traveled over the crags of Orla Perć in the Tatra Mountains—right after visiting Bronisław Maj during Margeret's first trip to Poland in 1993.

About the Author

Bronislaw Maj, born in Łódź, Poland, in 1953, since the 1980s has taught contemporary Polish literature at Jagiellonian University in Kraków. The author of several collections of poetry, he has won such major literary awards as the PEN Club Award for poetic achievement in 1995. During the mid-to-late 1980s, Maj was also the editor/director of *Na Głos* (Out Loud), a reading series in Kraków which served as one of the few "legal" literary forums available to the many Polish writers who chose not to belong to the government-controlled Polish Writers Union during the post-Martial Law period in the last decade of Communist Poland. The poems in this selection were originally published in Polish in the 1980s and 1990s in a number of books, starting with *Taka wolność (Such Freedom)*. But it was Maj's next two collections, *Wspólne powietrze (The Same Air)* and *Album rodzinny (Family Album)*—also published as Zagłada świętego *miasta (Extinction of the Holy City)*—that established Maj as perhaps the most significant poet of his generation, a reputation that continues to this day despite the fact that Maj has not published extensively in recent years. His work has also been translated into several languages, including in English in the literary journals *Salmagundi, Field, Seneca Review,* and *North American Review.*

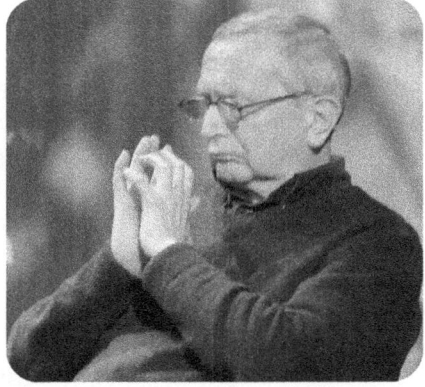

Photograph of Bronislaw Maj by Silar. Creative Commons Attribution-Share Alike 4.0 International license.

About the Translator

Daniel Bourne is the author of three books of poetry: *The Household Gods (Cleveland State University Poetry Center, 1995), Where No One Spoke the Language (CustomWords, 2006),* and *Talking Back to the Exterminator* Regal House, 2024)). His poems have also appeared in *Ploughshares, American Poetry Review, Boulevard, Guernica, Conduit, Salmagundi, Shenandoah, Prairie Schooner, Field, Michigan Quarterly Review, Plume, Yale Review,* and others. The founding editor of *Artful Dodge*, and the translation editor for its current online incarnation *The Dodge*, since 1980 he has lived off and on in Poland, including 1985-87 on a Fulbright for the translation of younger Polish poets, and most recently in 2018 and 2019 for work on an anthology of Baltic Coast poets. His translations of Bronisław Maj and other Polish poets have appeared in a number of journals, including *Field, Colorado Review, Partisan Review, Plume, Salmagundi, Beloit Poetry Journal, Boulevard, Virginia Quarterly Review, Prairie Schooner.* He also published a collection of selected political poems and essays of Tomasz Jastrun, *On the Crossroads of Asia and Europe* (Salmon Run Press), in 1999. The recipient of four Individual Excellence in Poetry Fellowships from the Ohio Arts Council, he taught in the English Department and Environmental Studies program at The College of Wooster from 1988 till 2020.

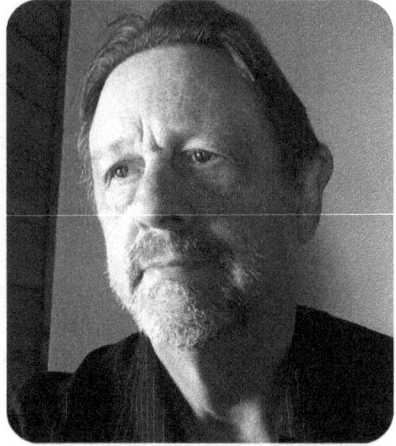

Photograph of Daniel Bourne. © Daniel Bourne. Used by permission.

About the Cover Artist

Wojciech Kołyszko is a leading Polish book designer and graphic artist. His work has appeared on the covers of numerous books in Poland and in the U.S., where his art has been on Czeslaw Milosz's *Facing the River: New Poems* (Ecco Press) and on several past covers of *Artful Dodge*. In recent years, he has become more active in working with children in art, nature, and mental health education, authoring many series of books and holding workshops throughout the country for children as well as teachers. His awards include The Polish Association of Book Publishers Prize for the best art book of the year in 1995, 1997 and 1999.

Free Verse Editions

Edited by Jon Thompson

An Unchanging Blue: Selected Poems 1962–1975 by Rolf Dieter Brinkmann, trans. by Mark Terrill
Under the Quick by Molly Bendall
Verge by Morgan Lucas Schuldt
The Visible Woman by Allison Funk
The Wash by Adam Clay
Well by Sasha Steensen
We'll See by Georges Godeau, trans. by Kathleen McGookey
What Stillness Illuminated by Yermiyahu Ahron Taub
Winter Journey [Viaggio d'inverno] by Attilio Bertolucci, trans. by Nicholas Benson
Wonder Rooms by Allison Funk

www.ingramcontent.com/pod-product-compliance
Lightning Source LLC
Chambersburg PA
CBHW021507090426
42739CB00007B/507